A POD OF GRAY WHALES

written and photographed by
François Gohier

Series Editor: Vicki León
Designer: Cathi Von Schimmelmann

© 1988 François Gohier and
Blake Publishing, Inc.
A division of

Graphic Center

2222 Beebee Street, San Luis Obispo California 93401.
Printed in the United States of America.
ISBN 0-918303-14-1

Although they are mammals like us, gray whales live in the ocean, an environment as huge, majestic and mysterious as they are. Because they come to the surface to breathe, we get an opportunity to see them. Or rather, to get tantalizing glimpses of them. We spot the white plume of a gray whale's blow on the ocean horizon. By the time we can focus on it, the shiny dark back of the whale has already slid into the deep. Sometimes the tail flukes appear, rising and expanding above the water like a blooming flower. And as we marvel over its perfect shape, the tail is gone, leaving only a whirlpool at the surface.

This is a book about the gray whale, believed to be the oldest of all the living species of whales. Despite its multimillion-year tenure on earth, we still know very little about the gray whale's life and behaviors. Perhaps that is part of the attraction for us.

The gray whale is one of ten different species of baleen whales that inhabit the oceans of the world. Among other characteristics, baleen whales differ from their distant cousins, the toothed whales, because they gather their food by straining it through bristly plates called baleen. Baleen whales are among the largest creatures on earth. They get their nourishment from some of the smallest creatures on earth – plankton, krill, small fish and crustaceans.

Reach out and touch: despite their slaughter to near-extinction twice in the last 120 years, gray whales seem to bear no malice. Certain whales approach their human visitors, letting us make more intimate contact with them.

Among the baleen species, gray whales weigh in as medium-sized. Adults get to be 40 to 50 feet long, as compared to 90 feet for blue whales. Grays can weigh 30 to 40 tons. Like other whales, they are covered with a layer of blubber six to 10 inches thick.

Their common name derives from their color. The skin itself is dark gray; it is mottled by white patches, scars and other marks and by colonies of light-colored parasites that make their home on the whale's snout and head.

Fifty million years ago, the ancestor of today's whale was a land mammal. It is still possible to find vestigial hind limbs of that far-off time in the gray whale's skeleton. Modern forms of whales have been present for more than 10 million years. We believe that the gray whale, a species well-adapted to the coastal habitat, has remained virtually unchanged during all that time.

For millions of years, gray whales roamed both the northern Pacific and Atlantic oceans unmolested. With man's coming, they began to be hunted. Archeological sites along the coasts of Siberia, Alaska and the Aleutian Islands show that grays have been pursued ever since man reached those shores.

Gray whale skeletons have been found on both sides of the Atlantic Ocean. In the New World, their bones have been unearthed from New York to Florida. One specimen from New York has been radiocarbon-dated to the 1670s. On the other side of the Atlantic, gray whale remains have been located along the European continent and in the British Isles. Early Basque, Icelandic and Yankee whalers were probably responsible for the demise of gray whales in the Atlantic.

In the Pacific Ocean, two distinct gray whale populations existed until recently. Now there is just one. The group that used to migrate between Siberia and Korea has been wiped out by whalers and is considered extinct or nearly so.

That leaves just the Pacific coast population. Twice in the last 120 years, this population has been brought dangerously close to extinction also.

Pacific coast gray whaling began in 1845. At that time, two ships spent the winter in Mexico's Magdalena Bay. There, whalers discovered the grays but soon found they were not easy prey. The harpooned animals were intelligent enough to identify their tormenters and often attacked the whaling boats, injuring or killing crew members.

Gray whales have an average life span of 50 years; an incredibly ancient species, the gray whale still has vestigial hind limbs in its skeleton.

Each year, gray whales make a 10,000-mile swim up and down the Pacific coast. Traveling in small groups called pods, they trace one of Nature's longest migratory paths.

Whalers began to develop a better knowledge of gray whales' movements and habits. The most disastrous consequence for the gray whale was the discovery of the secluded breeding and calving grounds in the lagoons of Baja California. Two of them were discovered between 1857 and 1860 by Captain Charles Scammon, one of which bears his name on American maps. From then on, the whalers operated at the heart of the gray whale breeding grounds. They had no qualms about using or killing the calves to attract and kill the frantic mother whales. In this fashion, the gray whales' numbers were reduced from an estimated 25,000 to a few thousand in 11 short seasons. After 1874, the stock was so depleted that few gray whales were taken.

A second onslaught came with the development of motorized whaling vessels and explosive harpoons. Between 1924 and 1946, another thousand gray whales were killed. This brought the already-scarce stock down to near-extinction levels.

What were the carcasses of the gray whales used for? First of all, it was oil. The average yield of oil from an adult was 20 barrels. Other products included baleen for women's corset stays. In the modern era, gray whales were routinely slaughtered for use as dog food.

In 1946, gray whales finally received official protection from commercial whaling.

There are several exceptions to this international ban: one for scientific purposes and another that permits up to 200 whales per year to be taken for consumption by the natives of northeastern Siberia.

Since 1946, the gray whale population has rebounded to a promising number. It is estimated that there may be as many as 18,000 living gray whales. This figure is extrapolated from a partial count, so a census is difficult. But it does seem that we have managed to contain ourselves in time to save one of the largest and noblest species with which we share this planet.

For millions of years, gray whales have migrated up and down the coast of North America, following an ancient ancestral rhythm.

Gray whales spend the summer in the Arctic. They range across the Bering Sea and even further north into the Chukchi Sea, along the coasts of Alaska and Siberia. What are they doing in this part of the world? Feeding. In the shallow parts of these seas, gray whales feed on small crustaceans called isopods and amphipods. These creatures live on the sea floor or in tunnels dug in the mud. The gray whale has a special technique for food gathering. It dives to the bottom, turns on its right side, opens its mouth slightly and sucks up a chunk of the bottom. The whale repeats this several times before surfacing to breathe. At

the surface, the whale filters out the water, debris and mud by pushing its tongue against the curtain of baleen in its mouth. What's left, trapped against the fibers of the baleen, are the crustaceans.

It is difficult to see gray whales feeding, but scientists have found oval-shaped depressions on the ocean floor, clear signs of feeding sessions. With this diet, gray whales put on tons of weight, most of it as stored fat. This reserve of energy will be needed during the long migration south.

A pod of grays in San Ignacio Lagoon gives their characteristic V-shaped blows. The dunes and mesa around the lagoon remain just as Captain Scammon saw them, over 100 years ago.

Most of the time, gray whales live in water where visibility is 20 feet or less.

Interestingly, not every gray whale goes all the way north in summer. Some of them linger along the coasts of northern California, Oregon, Washington and British Columbia. They have been observed feeding in the same manner and on the same kinds of prey as they would further north.

In the early fall, chilly winds begin to blow from the polar region. The days shorten, the ice reclaims the sea, and the gray whales move south. In November and December, they cross the chain of the Aleutian Islands at Unimak Pass, turn east and follow the coast of Alaska. By the thousands, they swim steadily along the Pacific coast. It is during that voyage that

Although the motives for it are not understood, breaching is the most spectacular behavior carried out by the gray whale. At the height of the breach, this whale may tower 30 or 40 feet out of the water.

most of the matings take place. At the end of December, the whales reach the Mexican waters of Baja California.

There they linger offshore or enter the shallow bays that dot the lower half of Baja: places known as Guerrero Negro Lagoon, Scammon's Lagoon, San Ignacio Lagoon and Magdalena Bay. The whales have left the blue-white world of the ice; now they are surrounded by the sugar-white of sand dunes. In these winter quarters they will spend several months mating, playing, giving birth and preparing their calves for the migration northward.

Once spring arrives, the grays will head north. This remarkable migratory pattern is one of the longest on record for any mammal. Some individuals travel more, some less, but the average figure is roughly 5,000 miles in each direction. The gray whale cruises at 4 to 5 knots (6 mph). They follow a course roughly parallel to the shoreline and stay in shallow water. Virtually all of the whales travel within the 50-fathom (300 feet) depth line, and most within the 20- to 30-fathom (120 to 180 feet) curve.

It was once thought that gray whales only fed during their Arctic summer. Thanks to recent observations, a different pattern has emerged. Grays gain most of their body weight at their northern feeding grounds, it's true. But it is also true that gray whales are opportunistic feeders in other parts of their range. If they run across schooling fish, surface plankton, pelagic red crabs or the small shrimplike creatures called krill, they will consume them also. Grays have

been seen eating kelp and eelgrass, which often shelter myriads of tiny animals. This openness to a varied diet may have helped the gray whales rebound as a species.

These animals spend most of the year in very turbid waters. Both the warm lagoons of Mexico and the icy waters of the Bering and Chukchi seas are filled with sand, sediment and tiny organisms. These bits of solid matter reduce underwater visibility to as little as 15 feet. Along the Pacific coast, where gray whales spend half their lives migrating, any diver will tell you that 45-foot visibility is very good indeed.

Gray whales have a moderately good sense of vision and use it to the maximum extent possible, both below the water's surface and above it. Which leads us to the most spectacular behavior in the repertoire of the gray whale – breaching.

Without warning, the enormous body of a gray whale comes out of the sea in front of our skiff. It shoots out of the water almost vertically, water spewing from the mouth, dripping from the flippers, shining in the sunlight. As the whale begins to fall down, its body pivots in the air and it crashes on its back, disappearing in a crater of white water. Seconds later, the whale jumps again, and then again.

In my years of whale watching, I have seen whales breach or leap out of the water repeatedly. Usually, gray whales jump two to five times in a row. Sometimes it seems that they will never stop. On one occasion, a whale jumped 21 consecutive times near the stern of our boat, which was anchored in San Ignacio Lagoon.

During breaching, about three-quarters of the whale's body comes out of the water. Since a gray whale can reach 40 or more feet in length, the whale towers as high as a multistory building during its breach. It is the most breathtaking display the animal makes.

Why do gray whales breach? No one has a definitive answer. Breaching occurs in varied circumstances. It has been seen near the long piers that extend into the sea from California beaches. It has been seen near passing boats, near skiffs in the Mexican lagoons, near or within courting groups of whales, near mother and calf pairs, and in the entrance channel to the lagoons.

Breaching often seems to be triggered by the presence of an object or obstruction. Some researchers believe that gray whales breach in order to see, or to avoid, an obstacle. Often the gray whale uses the momentum of its breaching jump to change course abruptly. The gray whale first detects the obstacle – such as a boat – by sound. Or perhaps by echolocation, a sonarlike mechanism used by dolphins but not yet proven to exist among baleen whales such as the gray.

But what should we make of the amazing series of jumps that we are sometimes lucky enough to observe? We are left with pure speculation. If a whale breaches more than 20 times near a boat, it certainly gets a good look at the vessel. Perhaps this is what the whale wants. The real motivation, however, may elude our understanding for a long time to come.

At the end of a breach, the gray whale falls back into the sea with a ponderous splash – up to 40 tons of animal.

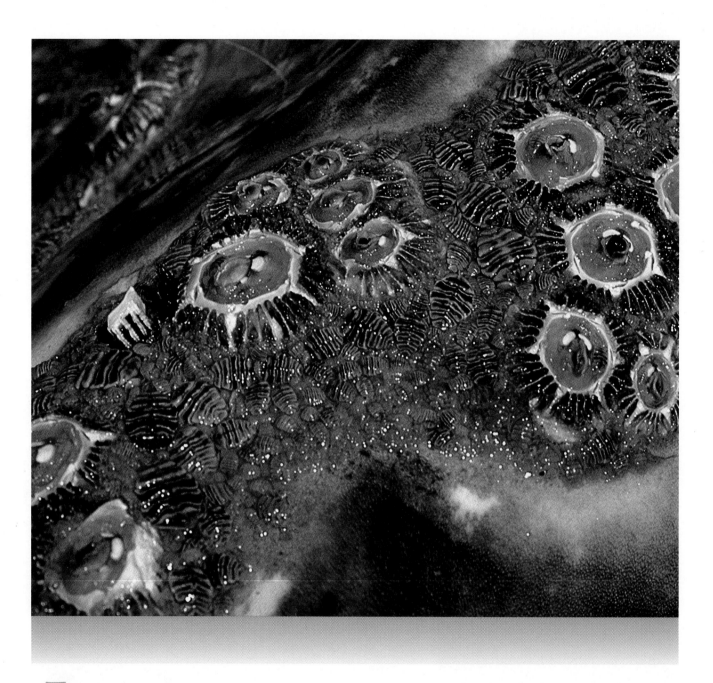

Another whale behavior that is a favorite for whale-watchers is "spyhopping." This is the term used when the head of the whale comes vertically out of the water for several seconds. The word implies that the whale is looking at its surroundings. Often, however, the eyes fail to come above the surface and the whale is not really looking at anything. The reasons for spyhopping are also unknown.

By sticking its head out of the water, the whale gives us a chance to see the other creatures that share its life: commensals such as the barnacle and parasites called whale lice. Soon after birth, the baby whale is infested with barnacle larvae and lice. The barnacles anchor themselves through the skin into the blubber and form very prominent colonies of distinctive white craters on the top and sides of the whale's head. Barnacles feed by filtering their microscopic food from the water. It is easy

to see the advantages of living on a gray whale, which spends much of its life in nutrient-rich waters. These barnacles belong to a species found only on the gray whale – another amazing fact reinforcing the idea that the gray is an ancient species and that the relationship has had ample time to develop.

Between the barnacles crawl enormous quantities of small pinkish crustaceans, the whale lice. The gray is host to three different species of these parasites, two of which, again, are found solely on the gray whale. If the animal dies and is washed ashore, the lice and barnacles die with the whale, their only viable world. Whale lice get as big as one-half inch in diameter and can bite cruelly. If the whale is injured, lice congregate in the wound and keep it clean by eating the decaying tissues. This is probably beneficial to the whale.

The most commonly seen behaviors of the gray whale are blowing and sounding. Because they are air-breathing mammals, gray whales

Hitching a ride: barnacles (top) and whale lice (shown twice life-size in middle of page) form firm attachments to gray whales. Their colonies give the whales a roughened appearance.

must periodically come to the surface. When they do, they exhale with great force through twin blowholes on the head. The warm, condensed air pushes sea water upwards, and this mixture forms a six- to 12-foot plume in the air, visible for some distance.

Like all cetaceans, gray whales receive most of the sensory data about their world through their hearing. They can also produce a variety of sounds, a talent that probably helps them find each other in the cloudy waters. Their sounds do not have the musical quality or variety of the humpback whale, whose long and strangely melodious songs have often been recorded. The most common gray whale noise is a burst of pulsing sounds lasting a few seconds. It can be crudely compared with the noise obtained by drumming on a gong: something like "BONG BONG bong bong." This pattern has been documented in all parts of their range. Gray whales also utter grunts, moans and other noises.

When the whale projects just part of its body vertically out of the water, it is called spyhopping. At left, the whale's throat is distended, as if the animal were swallowing.

Mating whales love
to touch. Their slow
courtship often involves
two males and one female.

Despite their bulk, gray whales possess a keen sense of touch. This becomes evident to the lucky observer who has a chance to see them courting, playing together or interacting with a foreign object such as a rubber dinghy. When lightly touched by a human hand, gray whales often shiver and back away. They usually return for gentle rubbing, and some even seem to enjoy brisker manipulation. I have seen them linger near the boat for long periods of time, savoring the massage they were getting from eager hands. In the Mexican lagoons, it is also possible to watch gray whales languorously rub against each other for hours at a time. They also seem to feel and enjoy the warm sun on their skin and will roll in the water as if basking.

During the winter months, courting and mating can often be seen in the lagoons of Baja California.

The process usually begins with up to 10 males following one female. Gradually, the number of males in pursuit drops to two. Apparently, it is not easy to be the size of a gray whale and to try to mate in an element as liquid as water. The whales go through phases of intense activity, with much thrashing of flippers and tails. These moments are followed by interludes of rest during which the three animals disappear underwater. They emerge again and the males position themselves alongside the female. As they roll, their flippers point toward the sky, coming down to gently touch the sides of the female. Time after time, the threesome tries to achieve intimate contact.

There is no visible aggression between the males, but both try to be successful. Eventually, one of them finds himself behind the female. He then seems to help her in keeping her balance while the other male can at last copulate. But the story does not end there. Courting play and mating continue for many hours. Both males generally get several chances to copulate. Sometimes the number will involve more than three whales.

Once the female becomes pregnant, the gestation period is believed to be 12 to 13 months. Most females calve every other year. A few calves are born at sea. Each year, some of them can be seen swimming bravely alongside their mothers off the coast of southern California. But most are born in Mexico in the remote and quiet upper reaches of the lagoons.

At birth, calves measure nearly 15 feet and weigh almost a ton. Their growth is rapid, sustained by a thick milk that contains nearly 55% fat.

In the 15-foot shallows, there is almost constant physical contact between mothers and calves. The calf swims at his mother's side, repeating virtually all her actions. When the mother stops to rest, however, the active little whale may find life a trifle dull. The calf will cross back and forth over the mother's tail and head, haul himself onto her back, bump into her side and tease her until she surrenders and plays with him.

Mother whale at its side, a young calf emits a junior-sized blow. Calves are born with the ability to surface and blow. Many other behaviors, however, must be learned.

The baleens are an overgrowth of the palate in the roof of the mouth. Hundreds of plates of this fibrous substance hang from the gray whale's jaw and strain the animal's food. Normally, there are no lice in a whale's mouth; the close-up below depicts a dead whale.

Tidal currents are strong in the lagoons. Sand bars and mud flats are alternately exposed and flooded. This makes the lagoons potentially dangerous for the calves. But by swimming against these currents, the young whales gain strength. By the time the calves are a few months old, they have moved with their mothers to the mouth of the lagoon. In April, they begin the long swim north to the Arctic.

"**T**har she blows!" has taken on a new meaning. Today's peaceful whale-watchers hunt with cameras and binoculars, not harpoons.

Today's gray whales are watched, not hunted. Brought back from the thin edge of extinction, the gray whale has become symbolic of the vast, mysterious and fragile marine resources of the Pacific coast. Its appeal is such that the gray whale has been designated the official marine mammal of California.

Among the great whale species, the grays are probably the most accessible for human observation. During their northern and southern migrations along the Pacific coast, they tend to hug the shore. The depth of the water in which they travel runs from 120 to 300 feet. The gray whales move at a stately pace, especially when headed north with young calves. Their nearness to shore, their pace and their numbers make them easy to find.

Fortunately for whale-watchers, the season to see the grays is long. The southbound migration begins in December and continues through January. A few stragglers may even be seen in February. The northbound migration begins about March and continues through May. This is the best time to see pods containing mothers and new calves. Naturally, the arrival times of each locale vary as the whales make their way north or south.

Good shoreline whale-watching places are numerous throughout California. Four of the primary spots are Mendocino, Point Reyes National Seashore, Point Lobos State Reserve and Cabrillo National Monument at San Diego. Excellent whale-watching from shore is also possible in Oregon, Washington, Alaska and British Columbia. The map on the inside front cover gives a list of locales, which is by no means exhaustive.

The gray whale has two to four distinctive grooves or pleats in its throat, right. Another characteristic of this whale are the bumps or knuckles along its back, shown top left.

Gray whales move in pods or groups of two to 10 animals. Their blows emerge from twin blowholes on the head. The grays tend to dive for three to five minutes at a time, coming up for a series of blows.

In many harbors up and down the Pacific coast, charter-boat companies offer whale-watching excursions during the times of peak migration. These low-cost excursions can last two to four hours and are often able to come thrillingly close to the grays without molesting the animals. Many whale-watching boat tours have a naturalist on board who gives a running narration and answers questions. Whale watching has in fact become a traditional winter activity in California.

A series of excellent marine museums and institutes along the Pacific coast also help curious humans learn more about gray whales. There may come a time, however, when these activities are simply not enough. Then it is time to take the ultimate whale-watching voyage: a week-long journey by boat to the lagoons of Baja California.

To see a gray whale from the shore or from a large whale-watching vessel is exciting. But to encounter and touch a gray whale in its natural environment is one of the most moving and extraordinary experiences in the world. As a naturalist and photographer, I have been privileged to lead many natural history trips to the Mexican lagoons where the gray whales spend the winter months. Season after season, these encounters continue to be charged with mystery and magic for me.

Such a trip to the Mexican breeding grounds of the gray whale begins in San Diego. Whale-watchers from around the world gather here for the weeklong voyages, most of which take place January through April. The vessels on which we travel carry about 30 passengers each.

Scientists used to believe that gray whales did not eat during their winter's stay in the lagoons of Baja California. Recent observations suggest that the grays may occasionally feed on what is available. The eelgrass that trails from this calf's mouth may contain crustaceans and other small food items. Above: the whale propels itself with its powerful tail flukes. The front flippers are used for turning and diving.

For two days we sail south from San Diego, landing at San Martín and San Benitos Islands for a close look at the wildlife on these rugged dots in the Pacific. Our cameras are filled with elephant seals, sea birds, osprey nests and colorful flowers. The third day, we slowly enter San Ignacio Lagoon, a body of water stretching 15 miles into the arid Vizcaíno Desert. To the east, a volcanic mesa makes a dark horizontal line. It looks exactly like the drawing made by Captain Scammon of the lagoon over 100 years ago.

To the northwest, a huge isolated sand dune towers over the hot desert. The light is intense, and the uncertain boundary between lagoon and sky shivers in a mirage.

From the mother vessel, we board our 15-foot rubber skiff and motor slowly across the lagoon. Fifty yards away, a whale seems to change direction. The skipper puts the engine in neutral and we wait.

Suddenly, an arm's length away, the head of the whale comes out of the water. The animal exhales in a powerful blow and everyone is sprayed with a mist of salt water. We cry out in surprise and excitement, but our cries don't seem to discourage the whale.

It sinks and comes up again. This time, the head touches the pontoon of the skiff. Hands quickly reach toward the whale to touch the wet, rubbery skin.

Later, another whale with a calf brings it to the skiff and allows it to be petted and gently stroked on the head. The baby whale can't seem to get enough of playing and touching. The passengers in the skiff are beside themselves. They laugh with delight as the calf pops out of the water, pushing the skiff with its head,

Whether they are moved by friendliness or curiosity, whales in the lagoons of Mexico sometimes seem to view their human visitors in rubber skiffs as toys. Here, a calf spyhops while its mother gives the skiff a lift.

letting us rub its smooth dark skin. Other adults and calves come near; rolling under the sun, rubbing one another, they surround the skiff. They look at us, eyes half-closed in the bright light of the surface. And we drift together in the lagoon, whales and humans sharing moments of confidence which would have been unthinkable in the past.

The first friendly whales (as they have become known) appeared during the winter of 1975-1976 in San Ignacio Lagoon. Until that time, boat skippers had kept a careful distance from the whales. It was believed that it was safer for both passengers and whales.

But apparently some of the gray whales were curious about their visitors.

They came to investigate the little buzzing objects, perhaps attracted by the motor noise or vibration. The whales obviously liked what they had found. In growing numbers, they have continued to approach humans.

The Mexican government enacted laws to protect the gray whales while in Mexican waters. Scammon's Lagoon and San Ignacio Lagoon are now official sanctuaries. Access to these Baja California lagoons while gray whales are in residence is strictly controlled. Only two boats at a time are allowed in the lagoon. No boats at all are permitted in the shallow waters of the upper lagoons, which the grays use as birthing areas and nurseries for the young calves.

In the not-so-distant past, encounters with humans meant terror, pain, death and near-extinction for gray whales. This senseless persecution has ceased and they may now see our approach as benign.

A few of these trusting, gentle animals have initiated a very different relationship with us. Perhaps they are wiser than we can know. By allowing us to have personal contact with them, the gray whales have become their own best ambassadors for survival. In the process, we have learned that they are fitting objects for our respect, wonder and love. ✖

Adult whales and calves alike approach peaceful human visitors to the secluded lagoons of Baja California. Gray whales are born with smooth, dimpled skin. Barnacles and lice soon form conspicuous colonies on the animals.

About the Author-Photographer

Writer-photographer François Gohier, whose work is presented on these pages, brings a wealth of background to the task. A French native, Gohier first studied nature photography in Paris and began working on assignment for magazines such as **GEO** and **La Vie des Bêtes** in 1973. His interest in gray whales was awakened by his work as a staff member for Lindblad Travel in 1976-77, which took him to all parts of the gray's range.

In 1979, he was invited to California by gray whale expert Dr. Theodore Walker, and subsequently spent most of the winter seasons between 1980 and 1986 photographing the gray whale in Mexico.

During this period, he also acted as guest naturalist for several boat companies doing whale tours.

Gohier's credits include such prestigious outlets as **National Geographic, Animal Kingdom, National Geographic World** and **Westways.** His work has also appeared in numerous European publications and in books such as the Abrams/Chanticleer Press Audubon series and Blake Publishing's **A Raft of Sea Otters.**

Acknowledgments

Nature photography is essentially a solitary activity. However, photographs of whales in the vast marine environment can only be obtained as the result of a team effort. For their assistance and advice over the years, I especially wish to thank: Dr. Carolyn R. Annerud and Dr. Theodore G. Walker.

I also wish to thank:
H and M Landing, San Diego: *Michael Keating, Judy Lobred, Phil Lobred, Dave McIntyre, Bob Miller, Catherine Miller, and Dr. Ralph Miller.*

National Geographic Society, Washington, D.C.: *William L. Allen, Neva L. Folk, Robert W. Hernández, and Mary G. Smith.*

Special Expeditions, Inc., New York: *Pamela W. Fingleton and Sven-Olof Lindblad.*

José María Aguilar, Marilyn E. Dahlheim, Robert Dahlheim, Janet Essley, Gail Roberts Fields, William S. Fields, José Francisco Mayoral González, Mary Lou Jones, and Steven L. Swartz.

For Further Information

Whale Center
3929 Piedmont Avenue, Oakland, CA 94611.
Phone (415) 654-6621.

Oceanic Society
Fort Mason Center, Building E, San Francisco, CA 94123.
Phone (415) 441-1104.

Greenpeace
Fort Mason Center, San Francisco, CA 94123.
Phone (415) 474-6767.

American Cetacean Society
P.O. Box 2639, San Pedro, CA 90731.
Phone (213) 548-6279.

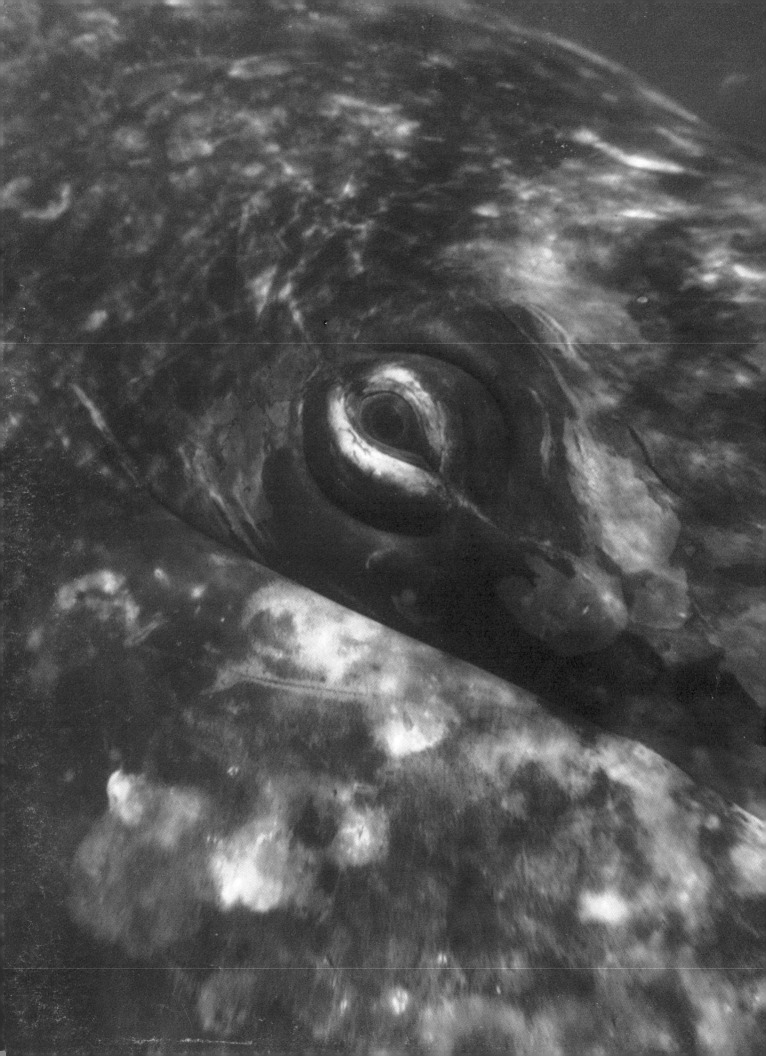